Greybeard's
Art of Self-Publishing

How to Publish Your Book and
Get It Out There Where People Can See It

Revision 2.0 – September 2019
Revision 2.1 – September 2020
Revision 2.2 – November 2021
Revision 2.3 – August 2024

David R. Beshears

Greybeard Publishing
www.greybeardpublishing.com

ISBN: 978-0-9969077-6-7

Greybeard Publishing
P.O. Box 480
McCleary, WA 98557-0480

Greybeard's
Art of Self-Publishing

Greybeard's Art of Self-Publishing

Appendices

A word from the author...

We set up an author booth at a few fairs and holiday bazaars each year, where I get a chance to sign some books, talk to folks about science fiction, fantasy, mountain climbing, just about everything but politics and religion.

During these events I'm often asked how to go about getting a book published, and I'm always happy to take them through it. I explain it all step by step, scribble notes and website links on the back pages of brochures.

But I'm always concerned that they walk away with their heads filled with dreams of self-publishing the great American novel, only to get home and recall maybe ten percent of all that wisdom I've laid on 'em.

So what I've tried to do with this guide is talk to you as I might talk to that fair goer. You and I are sitting there at my author booth and I'm explaining exactly how we publish our books, and how you can do the same.

But now when you walk away from my booth, you'll be taking this guide with you. As you work the process step by step, you will have this as a reference.

And I wish you all the luck in the world --
David R. Beshears

About this Guide

The purpose of this guide is to outline the steps you can take to self-publish your work. There are any number of paths to getting your book out there, some easier than others, some costly, and some free. We present here the path we choose with each title that we publish.

This guide will show you how to publish your titles in any ebook format, in print paperback and large print paperback, and in audiobook format.

And though this is not a marketing guide, we will touch upon a few marketing avenues and how to go about establishing your author presence. Such is a critical component of self-publishing and in getting your work out there.

There are a number of websites and companies mentioned throughout the guide. Links to all websites will be listed in the appendix at the end of the guide.

Update May 2017

We wanted to pass along to everyone several minor enhancements that we've made in our own publishing environment. These enhancements will be reflected in the new International Presence section in the Author Platform and the Amazon Marketing Services section in Online Marketing.

Update August 2019

This latest update reflects significant changes to the creation and publishing of the paperback edition of your title. CreateSpace, an independent publishing platform owned by Amazon, has been moved directly into Amazon, both ebook and paperback now residing in the Kindle Direct Publishing platform.

Revisions have also been made to marketing and several other sections.

Update September 2020

This revision includes minor changes / updates to the marketing section, reflecting explorations into new advertising options.

Update November 2021

This revision includes a section on producing and publishing hardcover editions.

Update August 2024

This revision includes additional marketing avenues, changes to author platform and link references.

A Brief History of Me

My name is David Beshears. I'm an award-winning author and screenwriter of science fiction, fantasy and adventure. I live on the Olympic Peninsula in Washington State with my wife, Sylvia. When not writing, I can usually be found on any one of a dozen northwest mountains.

Okay... It all started in a little town just south of San Francisco. I was twelve years old, which takes us back to the late nineteen sixties, where I was a sixth grader at San Andreas Elementary. Our teacher was rather progressive for her day; our classroom didn't have desks, we worked at tables, six students each. Each morning, she would write that day's assignments on the blackboard and we would work in teams to complete them. When finished, each student went to the back of the room and turned their card from red side to green side, and spent the rest of the day on extra credit.

One day I wrote a short story. When my teacher returned it to me the next day, she handed me an empty theme book and told me that from then on my only extra credit was to fill that theme book with stories.

How amazing was that? Teacher's orders... write stories.

Taking It from There to Here...

And I wrote a lot of stories after that. But I really didn't try to get anything published until I was well into my twenties, and then it consisted of typing three hundred page novels on a typewriter, putting them into the three inch cardboard boxes that reams of paper came in and mailing them off to big publishing houses, waiting for them to come back.

Yeah, unpublished authors didn't have it easy back then.

I only tried that a couple of times. I did get some great feedback, but none were willing to take a chance on an unknown science fiction writer. Good luck, dear author.

Later on, I did win some contests, mostly for my screenwriting, and I did get some short stories out there, and that was cool. All in all however, those early days were rather disappointing.

Then, back in the early nineteen nineties, I decided to publish my books myself. By then I was developing my own websites and I saw the Internet as a way to market my stuff; this was my first real inkling of getting my work out there all on my own.

Back then I had no thought of ebooks. That came later. Initially it was all about the print editions. Also back then, we saw our two options as either paying a printer for thousands of copies of each title, or printing our own. We chose to print our own. We bought the equipment: Printing, binding, laminating, cutting. The books came out great, but it wasn't cheap. Ink and materials added up. It was also very labor intensive.

We later found much better alternatives, which we'll be getting into in this guide.

Branding

We decided at the outset to publish as a small-press rather than as an independent author. Which way you choose to go is totally optional – most independent authors don't go the small-press route. Our reasoning was that we wanted to create branding. We wanted to publish under a publisher banner.

So... Greybeard Publishing.

Formatting

Like I said... originally it was all about the print editions. Since those early years, however, we've expanded into all formats: print, large print, all the ebook formats, and even audiobooks. And over the years, we've explored many of the venues available to produce and distribute these formats, and over that time we've come to have our favorites. We'll highlight some of these here.

Ebooks

As for ebooks... there's Kindle, and then there's the rest of the world.

We initially chose both, though we now publish ebook format exclusively through Amazon.

Prior to Kindle exclusive, we also published in multiple ebook formats through a site called Smashwords.

With Smashwords, once you've prepared and uploaded a manuscript, they will serve as your distributor. They publish in up to seven formats and send the title out through eighteen distribution channels, each in the proper ebook format for each channel. Sales on those sites route back to Smashwords and they send your royalties to you each month.

For most of those channels, you get about 60% royalties, some a little more, some a bit less. Smashwords charges a small transaction fee.

For Smashwords ebook formatting, I uploaded the manuscript in Microsoft Word's older .doc format. No headers or footers. On your copyright information page, include the phrase "Smashwords Edition". Remember also, your ebook will need its own ISBN. If you choose, Smashwords can provide one for you.

For Smashwords ebook editions, I used Times New Roman font for the body of the manuscript, and a bare minimum of special characters or alternate fonts.

I recommend downloading the Smashwords Style Guide from their website. It has all the information you need on formatting for their site, including the copyright page detail.

And then there's **Amazon Kindle**...

Yes, far and away the biggest market. And even though I'm one author among millions, the majority of my sales have always come through Amazon. I also find that I'm quite popular in the UK through the UK Amazon site.

You can publish your title directly through Amazon's Kindle Direct Publishing website or, if you are going to use Smashwords, you can choose to publish in Kindle format there and have them send it to Amazon.

When we used Smashwords, we elected to publish Kindle through Amazon directly and all other ebook formats through Smashwords, but that was because we started with Amazon with our first few titles and found Smashwords later. We were comfortable with keeping them separate. It also allowed for quicker updates to Amazon.

An important consideration when deciding on your ebook format is whether you want to take advantage of the exclusive features Amazon offers. If you want to use Amazon's free promotion program or place your ebook with Kindle Unlimited, you'll have to give Amazon exclusive rights to the digital format of your title. You can pull it out after 90 days if you wish, but while under exclusivity your book cannot be sold in any digital format other than Amazon's Kindle.

More on Kindle Unlimited and Amazon promotion features later in this guide.

If uploading your title directly to Amazon Kindle, they allow manuscripts in Word and other formats, but you really have to be careful about hidden characters and special formatting. They can play havoc with the final ebook.

For years I had used the Mobipocket Creator application to create .prc formatted documents from my manuscripts which I then uploaded to Amazon, which then converted the manuscript to .mobi (Kindle) format.

Amazon has stated they no longer support the .prc uploads and they want you to use their own tool. I have found that uploading Microsoft Word .docx files works great and now use this method exclusively. Amazon converts the manuscript and lets you know when it's ready to view.

Be sure to have the Kindle app on your computer. Always download the .mobi version and view in Kindle. If you find issues, make the necessary changes to the manuscript and upload the modified document.

Print (paperback)

Up until a few years ago my print (paperback) books were produced thru CreateSpace, an Amazon platform. Amazon has subsequently migrated the entire platform under the same umbrella as their Kindle platform, now called Kindle Direct Publishing (KDP).

There were some changes to paperback production, but these changes were minor.

You can set up your own formatting and upload the book's interior as a Microsoft Word manuscript. You can design your own covers, or you can pay to have it done. We do it all on our own, for free. We find the process to be straightforward, and the site will take you through it step by step.

For all our books other than our oversize Large Print editions, we choose the standard 6X9 size format. We use crème color paper for the interior for all fiction titles.

I submit my book interior in Microsoft Word's docx format. For these print editions, I use the Bookman Old Style font. Once you've uploaded the document, KDP's Interior Reviewer shows you what it will look like in a book and will highlight any errors.

We use the website's Cover Creator program for our book covers. With CreateSpace we always went with the "The Palm" design, but KDP no longer offers this. We have found an alternative design that works for us. With this design, you upload your own images for front and back cover. For the standard 6x9 size, cover image size is 6.25" x 9.5", and you'll want be sure you have at least a ½ inch outer boundary free of text and a space on the back cover for the UPC box. The Cover Creator takes you step by step through all of this.

Once your book's interior and exterior designs are completed and ready to go, you submit the book to the KDP process for review. It will let you know of any issues. Once it passes the site's review, you get to review the proof. You can download a digital copy or request a physical copy.

For our first CreateSpace title, we chose to have a print copy mailed to us, which gave us a chance to see what a physical copy actually looked like in hand. With all further titles we were comfortable with reviewing downloaded digital copies and have found no issues with KDP.

You will also decide the price and select the distribution options. They will present the minimum price you can set for your book, based on production cost per copy. You can plug in various test prices to see what you would receive in royalties through each distribution option.

If you do all the design on your own, there is no cost up front. KDP earns its money as your books are sold. They distribute my books to all the Amazon website platforms and through expanded distribution to a wide range of online retailers.

Royalties depend on the distribution avenue. In most cases you end up with anywhere from 40 to 60 percent, though with transaction fees you can end up with a lot less. With several European distribution avenues and some expanded distribution, a $12.90 book gets me like 73 cents. Yes, I can try to paint that all pretty and tell myself that it's a market that I would otherwise not reach, but it still kinda sucks. I mean, come on... 73 cents?

On average for my $12.90 priced books, I receive from about a $1 on the low end to as much as $6. An Amazon.com sale returns me on average $3.63 per book. The highest royalty comes from sales made directly through Amazon, so you'll want to provide the link to your book on their site to your customers.

I order print edition inventory from Amazon KDP at the production cost rate, and always keep enough copies of each title on hand to cover direct sales through my own websites as well as direct sales through several fairs and bazaars. My novellas run me $2 to $3 per copy, full size novels $4 to $5, and my oversize titles (such as large print editions) a little more.

Audiobooks

Most of my titles have recently gone to audiobook. We use ACX as our platform for producing and distributing our audiobooks. The ACX platform is where we search for the right narrator to produce each audiobook. Here is where contracts are created, communication with the narrator happens, and files get uploaded. The audiobook gets packaged here, and ACX distributes the audiobook to Amazon, Audible.com and iTunes.

Yes, ACX is yet another Amazon company.

You have two options when searching for and selecting a narrator/producer. You can pay the narrator a flat fee for their hours to produce the audiobook, or you and the narrator can share in the royalties. Up to now we've always gone the Royalty Share route. ACX takes 60% up front (this used to be 50%), and then we and the narrator split 50-50 the other 40%.

You start the process by putting your title on the site with an audition script and begin accepting auditions. Narrators read your audition script and post it for you to listen to. Once you find your narrator and come to an agreement, the narrator will produce and upload chapter audio files for you to review. You go back and forth as necessary until you're happy. You then upload a cover to ACX, and then let ACX put it all together. Once done, it gets shipped off to Amazon, Audible.com and iTunes.

For our audiobook covers, we usually crop our original book covers and adapt them to 1200x1200 pixels. This way all formats of our books have the same look.

Hardcover Editions

We began publishing our titles in hardcover format in January 2021. We chose IngramSpark as the platform, utilizing their distribution channels to get our books into numerous locations. Note that while they offer to include our titles in their newsletters for a fee, we've chosen not to take them up on it; haven't seen the need to now.

You select cover design, hardcover style, interior paper (we highly recommend crème for fiction), font style, chapter header design and so on; lots and lots of choices at all stages of design.

Your hardcovers will each need their own ISBN.

You can also publish in ebook format through IngramSpark, but for now we're sticking with Amazon Kindle for that format, as we're going with Kindle Unlimited.

Amazon recently added hardcover production option. Our current understanding is they have very limited distribution options compared to IngramSpark.

Copyrighting

Literary work is considered copyrighted the moment it is created. However, should there be a legal question, an author has a much better chance of winning if the work has been officially copyrighted.

Back in the olden days, I had to print out a copy of the manuscript, package it up with the copyright application, include a check, and mail it off.

It is much easier nowadays. You simply go online, fill out the application and click a button to upload your manuscript. The whole thing takes a couple of minutes and it's all done. The cost is $35.

Make sure you actually go to the official .gov site (find the link at the end of this guide). There are websites that look totally official, but with most all they're doing is taking your stuff and uploading it to the copyright site for you, charging you a handling fee. That's cool, I suppose, if you're okay with that, but it's not necessary.

ISBNs

An ISBN is an International Standard Book Number, and this is where you can incur some cost upfront.

If a title has both an ebook edition and a print edition, each will need its own ISBN. If you come out with a Large Print edition, it will also need its own ISBN.

Bowker's ISBN website: https://www.myidentifiers.com. Until recently I had been buying ISBN numbers in blocks of 10 at a cost of $295 per block. I wish now I had originally bought a set of 100, which would have saved me a lot of money (100 goes for $575). So, ISBN numbers at $29.50 each in a block of ten, or $5.75 each in a block of 100.

When Bowker had a two-day sale a while back, I finally caved and bought a 100 block at $450. I couldn't pass it up. It was a great deal when compared to buying them ten at time.

You can also buy them one at a time, but then it gets a whole lot more expensive: $125 each. Ouch.

There is a free avenue to your ISBN. If you're okay with having your ebook title under the Smashwords ISBN umbrella, you can get it for free at the time you post your book on their site. Other publishing avenues offer something similar for the print edition, although there are usually distribution limitations.

I wanted the ISBNs of all my titles under the Greybeard Publishing brand, so I bought my own. This way my own imprint is reflected during ISBN searches and on the detail pages of my books on retail websites. You see this on Amazon's book detail page for instance.

If you choose to use your own, register with Bowker ahead of time so you'll have your ISBN info ready. You will also want to enter your ISBN into your manuscript before uploading it to the publishing sites. It should go on the copyright page of your book. And remember, each format gets its own ISBN.

Steps to Publishing your Book

As a review, here are the steps involved when we take a title from manuscript through to market.

1. Edit manuscript – *final edit, ahead of adapting to various formats*

2. Copyright manuscript

3. Design covers – front and back covers

4. Assign ISBNs for each format (via Bowker)

5. Create manuscript documents for Smashwords, Amazon Kindle Direct Publishing (kindle and paperback); *include ISBN numbers on copyright pages*

6. Create prospectus document – book description, author info, etc.

7. Create blog info document – descriptions to post onto blogs, author page, social media posts

8. Outline marketing campaign

9. Publish ebook format to Amazon Kindle

10. Publish paperback using Kindle Direct Publishing

11. Publish hardcover using IngramSpark

12. Publish to Smashwords (optional, and only if not going Kindle exclusive)

13. Post info on websites, blogs, social media sites

Choosing Kindle Exclusive

A major decision you'll have to make when it comes to publishing the ebook format of your title is whether to go with Amazon Kindle exclusive.

On the face of it, you might ask *'why would I want to do that?'*

Good question. Why give it all to Amazon? Why not also publish to Apple, Barnes & Noble and all the others?

Well, Amazon does offer some, uh... encouragements.

If you agree to place the ebook format of a title exclusively with Amazon, you then have the option of several promotion programs, including their free promotion. While we no longer use it, the free promotion definitely gets a title out there. With each promotion, we saw hundreds, sometimes several thousand copies downloaded. Some of our titles temporarily reached number one on Amazon in their genre or category. If you can tie a promotion to another book, such as a series, it can be worthwhile.

Also, more recently, there is Amazon's Kindle Unlimited (KU) program, available to you only if your title is Kindle exclusive.

Sometime back, we noticed a sudden drop-off in Kindle sales of our titles. At that time, we were selling ebook formats of all our titles through many different distribution routes, including B&N and all the others. However, most of our actual sales were Kindle. It wasn't even close. So the sudden drop-off hurt.

After some research, we found that the drop-off in Kindle sales occurred right about the time that this new program called Kindle Unlimited was taking off. With this program, members of Kindle Unlimited can read as many books as they like for a flat monthly fee. Amazon takes a chunk of all customer monthly fees, and the rest is divided up amongst all authors based on how many total pages of all books were read that month through KU.

If your book isn't in the program, you have to rely on traditional sales, and we found that a lot of customers had begun going with Kindle Unlimited over traditional purchases. If a customer can download another author's book for free, why pay $3.45 for yours?

So we migrated several of our titles over to Kindle exclusive and joined KU. We almost immediately saw our sales begin to climb back up for those titles. Additionally, in some cases, a Kindle Unlimited "sale" earns more than a traditional sale for the same title.

Ebook format for all of our titles are currently Kindle exclusive.

Be aware that when you agree to place a title Kindle exclusive, it doesn't have to be forever. You give them 90 days, and you can cancel after that time if it isn't turning out the way you want. Then just republish your title on Smashwords, get it back out there to other distribution routes.

Also note that the exclusivity you grant Amazon is only with the digital format of your title. You can continue to offer print (paperback and hardcover) and audiobook formats wherever you like.

Marketing

If you don't market what you publish, nobody is going to read what you write.

There. I said it.

While I would rather spend all my time writing, alas, no.

Author Platform

You need to create and nurture an author presence. This presence needs to address and serve several key elements. The folks out there need to be able to find you. When they find you, they must see you as a professional, approachable writer they feel comfortable and confident giving their money to in exchange for your creations. And the author presence should make it quick and easy to find and purchase what you are offering.

Your author presence must absolutely include an author website. Your website should show the world who you are, what you're offering, why they should buy what you're offering, and make it easy to do so.

We maintained our own web server and author and publisher websites for many years, but now keep our sites on GoDaddy; not nearly as versatile as developing myself, but clean, low maintenance, and allows me more time for writing.

There are other website placement options out there, WordPress for example, but GoDaddy seemed to fit our needs quite well.

If you're going to sell on Amazon, and you should, then you will need an Amazon author page. Your Amazon author page introduces you to your audience and presents the titles you have listed on Amazon (print, ebook and audiobook). You can also include images and videos, reviews and more. You create your Amazon author page at Author Central (link at end of this guide). All the titles you offer on Amazon will display on your Amazon Author Page, the different formats of each title listed together under each title.

Next, you should definitely use Goodreads. Many readers live here, and they talk to one another. Become an author on the site and place your books there. You can participate in their book giveaways, which helps let Goodreads folks see you and perhaps you can gain a few reviews of your books. Also encourage those outside of Goodreads to leave reviews not just on Amazon but also on Goodreads. You can also utilize the Goodreads author blog and other author tools on the site.

You should use social media: Facebook, Google+, etc...
I admit that I'm less comfortable here than with my
author pages, but I know how important these are. I
don't always see immediate correlations between my
day-to-day activity on these sites and direct sales
unless I'm in the midst of a marketing campaign, but
while in a campaign the audience is already familiar
with my name and they are more likely to take a
second look. I also believe that familiarity makes me
more approachable.

I have chosen to keep my author platform presence
social media primarily professional, only rarely posting
anything personal. Those personal posts, when I do
make them, are intended to give my audience a
positive window into who I am. I take them on one of
my hikes or one of my other adventures, and show
them what inspires me.

I have two Facebook accounts: author page and
personal. My Facebook Author Page is strictly author
focused, while my personal page may get an
occasional pic of our animals or of family. Note that
my personal page does allow glimpses into my
personal life, but it is nonetheless a component of my
author presence and I never, ever forget that.

And finally, I created an author blog website. I use the
posts to keep my fans up-to-date on the progress of
my writing projects. The posts are more informal than

other interactions, though I still keep them professional.

While I created my blog site from code, there are free tools available out there such as WordPress.

International Presence

If you're selling books on Amazon, then you're selling books on Amazon sites all over the world. At the time of this writing, most of these other flavors of Amazon don't as yet offer the ability to create an Author Page, but Amazon UK does. In the same way that you create an Author Page on Amazon.com, you should similarly use the Amazon UK Author Central to create an author page on their site.

We regularly monitor our presence on a number of the English speaking Amazon websites, including Amazon UK, Amazon Australia, Amazon Canada and Amazon India.

Online Marketing

Two of the most popular online marketing venues are Facebook Ads and Google Ads (I'll address Amazon Ads in a minute). I've had some success with Facebook, less so with Google Ads.

Facebook Ads can be placed along the side of screen (right column), or in the feed. I've had greater success with feed placement. With both, you create an image ad, 1200 x 600 pixels. Note that only 20% of the ad can contain text. Ad creation is pretty straightforward. You define your image, description and link, campaign schedule, and your target audience.

I have also recently begun using **Bookbub**, a popular platform offering ebooks to its large audience. There are also several marketing features available to publishers. I hesitated using Bookbub in the past as some of its advertising options can be expensive, but a couple of years ago they launched "BookBub Ads for Authors". These ads are included in their daily emails.

You create your ads via a campaign. Select your book, enter 10-60 characters of text, add your book cover and choose a button (i.e. "Buy Now"). Finally, define your audience and set up your campaign schedule and budget. I have all my books in the campaign and cycling the titles, letting each run for 5-7 days. I use the Cost per Click (CPC) and a daily total for each title. I suggest starting small and monitor how it goes. You can pause, edit, copy ads at any time, so play with it.

While you're establishing yourself as a Goodreads author on the Goodreads site, also take some time to explore creating a Goodreads ad. I haven't used their more expensive service, but I have placed a number of the small ads on their website in the past. I used thumbnail images of my books with a few lines of description, include either an Amazon link or the link to one of my own websites. You can set up a campaign, bid what you're willing to pay and for how long. Again, the cost to test your return on investment is minimal.

Goodreads also has a Goodreads giveaway program. You as an author offer up a number of paperback editions of your book. The giveaway lasts for the number of days that you specify, after which Goodreads draws winners. You send out the copies.

I've done the giveaway a few times. I didn't see much of a jump in sales over in Amazon for any of them, but I have gotten a few reviews out of it, usually only on Goodreads. The cost is only that of however many books you give away and the shipping. I usually choose to give away five copies.

As I noted earlier in this guide, Amazon has a Free Promotion program available for Kindle titles in which Amazon has exclusive digital rights. This program allows you to give copies away for 1 to 5 days every 90 days. Once you set the date range, head out to any number of free promotion sites to advertise the upcoming event. Many charge a fee, many others don't.

While we no longer do the free promotions, when we did we focused on fifteen websites that promote your promotion for free. Google 'free ebook promotion' and you'll return hundreds. Some we've gone with include FreeBooksy, Reading Deals, eBook Lister, Kindle Book Promos. There are also services that will place your promotion on all the sites for a fee, but we never went that route.

One word of caution regarding giving ebooks away for free...

When someone pays for a book, even if it is only 99 cents, they tend to read the description before buying. Not so when a book is free. Many folks click every free book download link they see, without looking to see whether it is the type of book they would be particularly interested in. They don't fully read the promo ad, and certainly don't read the book's description. They see the promo for a free book and click the link.

This can have a downside.

My books usually receive ratings of 4 or 5 stars (thank you all very much!). However, we have received some 3 star ratings. We found that just about every one of these lesser ratings came directly on the heels of a free book giveaway. Someone downloads a book they would otherwise have no interest in, so their view of that book isn't all you'd hope for.

So, be forewarned. This may or may not happen to you.

Now... Amazon Ads.

Amazon Ads has become my primary marketing tool, and is the method that has provided me the greatest return on investment.

The platform is called Amazon Marketing Services, where you design your own ad campaign. They offer two campaign types.

With Sponsored Products, you select the book you want to promote, enter a date range, specify your daily budget, your bid on cost-per-click for each keyword. Enter search keywords or automatic targeting, enter up to 150 characters of custom text for the ad and you're ready to go.

I recommend that you monitor your ads regularly and tweak your bid per click for each keyword up or down based on page impressions.

Whereas a sponsored product ad focuses on an individual book, Amazon's Sponsored Brand option showcases you as an author. We had used it in combination with the product ads in the past, but have focused on the individual book ads over the last few years.

However, Amazon now offers a Sponsored Brands Video option. Videos are limited to 45 seconds, and there are a number of general requirements, such as website addresses outside Amazon, etc. We created a brand video using one of our YouTube videos, modifying it to meet Amazon's guidelines and directing viewers to our Amazon Author Page via the link click. We can verify that it does generate additional interest to our brand. Sales to date have only marginally increased, and so we are looking at possible tweaks and adjustments to target audience selections. Note that you will definitely want to have an appealing Amazon Author Page to send the viewer to.

Direct sales

We have found that most of our sales of print and large print sales come from direct sales through my author booth at fairs and bazaars. Only a small percentage of paperback sales occur online, and most of these are through our Greybeard Publishing website. One exception is overseas sales. We do have an ongoing trickle of paperback sales through Amazon's European and UK websites.

So we tend to focus on local fairs holiday bazaars for our paperback sales. This is also an opportunity for potential long-term fans. I talk with fair goers about writing, publishing, science fiction, mountain climbing... we give out book catalogs, get involved in the venue's giveaways by donating books. And of course I sign a lot of books.

And it's an opportunity for me to look up from my computer monitor for a day or two, and as I said, to meet and make new fans.

As for the Greybeard Publishing website, while it is online I do tend to refer to it as direct sales. We post news and info on the site, run special events, offer various bundles, signed copies, etc. Through this and my official Author Page, we work hard to establish a relationship with our audience.

Appendix A:
Links to all the Websites

Links to websites mentioned in this guide:

ACX *(Audiobook Creation Exchange)*
   www.acx.com

Amazon Author Central
   https://authorcentral.amazon.com

Amazon Marketing Services
   https://ams.amazon.com/ads/dashboard

BookBub Partners
   https://partners.bookbub.com/

Bowker, Identifier Services - ISBN
   www.myidentifiers.com/get-your-isbn-now

Facebook business
   www.facebook.com/business

GoDaddy
   www.godaddy.com

Goodreads
   www.goodreads.com

Google Adwords
   www.google.com/adwords

IngramSpark
   www.ingramspark.com

Kindle Direct Publishing
  https://kdp.amazon.com

Smashwords
  www.smashwords.com

U.S. Copyright Office
  (select "How do I register a copyright")
  www.copyright.gov

WordPress
  https://wordpress.com/create

Amazon International

Amazon UK
  https://amazon.co.uk/

Amazon Australia
  https://www.amazon.com.au/

Amazon Canada
  https://www.amazon.ca/

Amazon India
  https://www.amazon.in/

Appendix B:
David's Author Presence

Where you can find the author:

Official Author Page
   www.davidrbeshears.com

Greybeard Publishing
   www.GreybeardPublishing.com

Amazon Author Page
   http://amazon.com/author/davidbeshears

Facebook Author Page
   www.facebook.com/davidrbeshears

Goodreads
   www.goodreads.com/drbeshears

Barnes and Noble
   www.barnesandnoble.com/c/david-r.-beshears

LinkedIn
   http://lnkd.in/HZQK6K

YouTube
   https://www.youtube.com/@davidbeshears/videos

Instagram
   https://www.instagram.com/drbeshears_author/

Find more links on
   www.davidrbeshears.com